The Runaway Soccer Ball

by Amanda Stiles
illustrated by Richard Torrey

SCHOLASTIC INC.

New York • Toronto • London • Auckland
Sydney • Mexico City • New Delhi • Hong Kong

ISBN 978-0-545-68612-9

Copyright © 2010 by Lefty's Editorial Services.

All rights reserved. Published by Scholastic Inc.

SCHOLASTIC, LET'S LEARN READERS™, and associated logos
are trademarks and/or registered trademarks of Scholastic Inc.

12 11 10 9 8 7 6 5 4 3 2 1   14 15 16 17 18 19/0

Printed in China.

Nancy loved soccer! She loved it so much, she never wanted to do anything else.

One day, Nancy was practicing some moves when...OOPS! She accidentally kicked her soccer ball into the schoolyard.

PREDICT

What do you think Nancy might do next?

Nancy ran after the ball. It rolled into the middle of a basketball game.

"Hey, we need another player," said Sam. "Will you join us?"

Nancy wanted to be nice, so she said
yes. Wow, basketball was fun!

**How many kids are playing
basketball?**

Nancy played for a while, then...OOPS!
One of the kids accidentally kicked her
soccer ball.

Nancy ran after the ball. It rolled under a jump rope. "Hey, we need a new jumper," said Allison. "Will you join us?"

QUESTION

Do you think Nancy will join in?

7

Nancy wanted to be nice, so she said yes. Wow, jumping rope was fun!

Do you like to try new things? Why or why not?

Nancy jumped for a while, then...OOPS!
One of the kids accidentally kicked her
soccer ball.

Nancy ran after the ball. It hit a bench, where some kids were practicing a play.

"Hey, we need another actor," said Leo. "Will you join us?"

Nancy wanted to be nice, so she said yes. Wow, acting was fun!

 INVESTIGATE **Look at the picture. What is Nancy pretending to be?**

Nancy acted for a while, then...OOPS!
One of the kids accidentally kicked her
soccer ball yet again.

Nancy ran after the ball. It bumped against a wall, where some kids were painting a mural.

"Hey, we need another artist," said Maya. "Will you join us?"

Do you like art? What do you like to paint or draw?

Nancy wanted to be nice, so she said yes. She picked up a brush and began to paint. Wow, art was fun! In fact, it was really, really fun.

Nancy put her ball in a place where nobody could kick it. Soccer would always be her favorite activity. But it was great to try new things!

TIE UP

What lesson did Nancy learn?

Story Prompts

Answer these questions after you have read the book.

1 Can you retell this story in your own words?

2 Do you think Nancy will continue to try new things? Why or why not?

3 What is your very favorite activity? Tell a story about it.